Tap In
Not Out

How overwhelmed moms can reclaim
peace, cultivate a better life, and thrive

Brittany Churchill

ISBN: 978-1-7343788-0-1

Dedication

This book is dedicated to my son, Ellis, and my daughter, Brecklyn. Without you both, I would not have these stories to share, and without you I would not be the person I am today. You have truly made me a better human being. I love you.

FREE STUFF!

DOWNLOAD
THE BOOK JOURNAL
PLUS
FIVE INSPIRATIONAL PRINTABLES
FOR FREE!

I just want to say thank you for buying my book. All the hearts to you, my friend! My hope is that this aids and supports you in your journey toward a thriving motherhood.

I believe in you, girl!

So much love,
Brittany

DOWNLOAD THE JOURNAL HERE:
http://bit.ly/tapinnotoutfreejournal

God is not a causeless God.

—Alicia Britt Chole

Contents

Introduction

Let's be honest. You don't have time for this book. Chances are you have a voicemail from last week and a few text messages from God knows when that you still need to return. And you probably have a heap of clean laundry sitting on a chair that should have been put away last Wednesday. Or like me, the same load of laundry is still sitting in the washing machine and needs to be washed for the third time this week. With all the high tech sensors on appliances and cars, you would think it would be standard by now to have a washing machine sense the smell of mildew and sound off an alarm to remind us overextended, forgetful parents to switch the laundry.

If this sounds like your life, I get you. I've had the greasy, messy bun days, the awkward postpartum body, and the unnoticed yogurt and spit up on my outfit while grocery shopping moments. I've juggled the full-blown toddler tantrums at Target, the frantic insertion of boob to starving mouth in public, and yes, I've peed my pants while jogging, jumping, and sneezing. Some moms call this time of life a beautiful mess. I call it gloriously insane.

I remember soaking up all the advice I could get during my first pregnancy. I thought I felt ready for this grand life change. In fact, I expected to walk gracefully into my life's calling as soon as my son entered this world. But that's far from what happened.

I quickly found out how to survive the chaotic days with chocolate cake and other indulgences, but I realized that it still left me wanting. With a sugar addiction and a restless need for more out of life, I made my way to better health and searched for answers that kept my soul thriving. The journey wasn't straightforward, but each step brought me closer to a more satisfying life—I just had to choose to tap in instead of out.

LIMITING BELIEFS

CHAPTER 1
I Don't Need Faith to Wipe Butts

I sat on the toilet and held my pee-covered stick. The color in my face drained away slowly as I stared at those two bright pink lines and tried to wrap my mind around the reality. *We wanted this*, I thought, trying to convince myself. *But now I have to push a person out of my body. A sweet lump of flesh, bones, and brains will absolutely need to come out of me somehow.* I winced at the thought. Time passed. Still terrified, I shared my big news with friends and family and they all rejoiced. Congratulations, gifts, and advice followed soon after. Every mom friend raved about *What to Expect When You're Expecting*, the legendary, must-read book with multiple new editions withstanding time and generational relevance. Praise be for this book. So I bought it. It was easy to see why most moms latched onto this book. It was like a mother of manuals answering all the major questions surrounding pregnancy. It laid out all the information I needed in organized sections based on each trimester. With my pregnancy playbook in tow, I felt more prepared for the next nine months.

But in all of my readings, I had made an assumption—I don't need faith to wipe butts. Security came with the knowledge I was amassing. The future looked pretty clear. At home, the basic things like changing diapers I broke down into a 1-2-3 step process. Raising a baby sounded pretty straightforward. In fact, I skipped the recommended pregnancy class because I was so confident. I knew that women's bodies were made to give birth to children. And my primary instincts to be a nurturing mother would swoop over me just as naturally as a first-time mother robin. I'm pretty sure she didn't go to a birdhouse meeting with her man Robin to discuss the importance of nest building, keeping the eggs warm, and feeding only soft mushy worms to the babies until they reach a certain age. She had a mother's instinct, and I was sure, even on some animalistic level, that I did too. Women have been birthing humans for thousands of years. I have all the right lady parts, so I should be good to go.

And then labor came two weeks early. Unexpectedly, my water broke when I got up to pee at one o'clock in the morning. My hospital bag was not packed, the crib was not put together, and I had multiple pre-baby commitments that weekend. This I was not prepared for. My confidence eventually flat lined somewhere within the thirty-eight hours of induced labor. It was a blur. Even though my water broke, my body did not go into labor. Three rounds of Cytotec and I was not quite ready for Pitocin. They started an IV anyway. An anesthesiologist walked in soon after and poked my back. I felt something zap my right hip. *That's not right. I'm pretty sure I should feel nothing.* Within the hour the room was sweltering. I asked them to switch the AC to blast the coldest air possible, but I was still sweating. I kept hitting the epidural booster in vain, trying to prevent the back pain from stretching further around my right side. The pain was constant, nauseating. I thought for sure I was going to die. At this rate, I doubted my baby would be on the outside of my body when I did. I pleaded with God to help me. My faith was in my God-designed body to do its thing, but my lady parts appeared to have hit a glitch. I thought my body had malfunctioned. I had no idea how to breathe right, and I tossed in a pool of regret for not going to any of those darn pregnancy classes. With desperate eyes, I pleaded with the young nurse bringing me ice chips, a delicacy at this point, to give me a crash course on how to get through this. Her words, "Find a spot on the wall and think happy thoughts." My thoughts—*how about I throw some ice chips at your unempathetic, happy face?* Thankfully, the new anesthesiologist, Dr. Dreamy, walked in after a shift change and adjusted my epidural. Within seconds, my pain was completely gone. I cried and called him my hero. At this point, I resembled a beached whale because of all the fluid retention and my body shakes had tripled in intensity. Flattering. The nurse checked me and to my disbelief, it was time to push. I made it to the final one hundred meter dash. My doctor rolled a mirror around so I could watch myself push. Embarrassed, I turned away immediately, not wanting to catch myself accidentally pooping with every push. Like a drill sergeant, she commanded me to focus and push for the next two and a half hours. Miraculously, my son was born, and I was terrified. Don't get me wrong, I was thrilled to meet him and even more so relieved that he was out of my body healthy and whole—but I was mostly panicky. You would think I would have seen the sign that I was about to walk into a life that I knew nothing about. Regardless of how many people walked this path before me and how instinctual mother nature might be, I was in for the greatest life-altering experience.

After a couple of days recovering in the hospital, we received the big thumbs up to be released. I double-checked with the discharge nurse if she honestly thought I was prepared enough to go home because I didn't see any sign of motherly instincts kicking in. She assured me and gave me the postpartum pep talk. I started making my mental checklists as she spoke— random crying is normal, feeling overwhelmed is normal, feeling unable to be a good mom is normal. Her words were both comforting and alarming. My mind was racing, interrogating my soul with questions like— *What did I just get myself into? I chose to do this? Why did I think I was ready to do this?* At this point, there wasn't any choice but to move forward and embrace the newness of it all. I had my child-rearing manuals to reference if I needed help or I could phone a friend. My resources were easily accessible. To encourage myself, I recalled that women have been doing this for years, and I'm not a barbarian, so the odds of success were fairly good. No divine intervention needed. The path seemed pretty well paved from this point on. So I put my big girl hospital panties on—you know the stretchy ones that go up past your belly button—and took my precious baby boy home like it was my job.

That was my mindset—motherhood was a job. It required feeding humans, teaching them about the world, and creating sleep schedules. It was a way of life. You just do it. If your baby is hungry, you feed him. If he is tired, you rock him. If he poops, you wipe his butt and give him a clean diaper. These tasks don't warrant a heavenly intervention. It just seemed all a part of the description of being a parent, you know? There didn't seem to be anything other-worldly or spiritual about taking care of somebody. You just did it like you do any type of work. And any connection I had with God was outside of this mundane booger cleaning job.

But apparently, I sucked at this.

CHAPTER 2
I Suck

Or so I told myself regularly. Even though I boasted about my resources and parenting plans, I entered motherhood with subconscious limiting beliefs that colored how I viewed my job performance.

The mom guilt began before I even pushed a kid into this world and then it snowballed with every milestone. I was only twenty-five when I got pregnant. I was thin. I gained sixty pounds during my first pregnancy, not for everyone's amazement and entertainment, but mostly because I craved cheeseburgers. I also blame my sturdy, Scottish genetics. People would say,

"Oh, I can't believe you're already showing!"

"You look like you're about to pop!"

"Are you having triplets? Are you sure you only have one baby in there?!"

The shaming, passively or actively, hurt. I walked into work the day after my five-month prenatal appointment. My boss, knowing that I was dreading the number on the scale that would be documented forever in my medical chart, asked me openly in front of others, "So how much did you gain?" With sad eyes and clear self-disapproval, I said, "I've gained thirty pounds."

She burst into laughter. Genuine laughter.

Apparently, it's amusing to watch someone thin struggle emotionally with gaining a lot of weight really fast. Being a pregnant spectacle catapulted me into the *I suck at this mode.*

That mindset snowballed further during labor when I had conceded that my body wasn't made for childbirth. Exhausted, I latched onto my slimy newborn's body and held him for the first time. I felt timid and unsure. We greeted each other with our eyes. I kissed him and welcomed him to the world. Then I waited for the gush of love to swoop over me, bonding me deeply with my little boy. It did not come. *Why didn't I feel that instant gush of love for my baby like everyone had told me I would? I must be a terrible mom.*

Our bond grew over the following weeks, and I learned how common it is to have a delayed bond with your newborn. That made me feel a little better or at least normalish.

After four months of scheduling feedings and making sure he had everything he needed, I assumed we would get a great report from the doctor when we showed up for his well-child check that month. When we arrived for the appointment, the nurse took all the usual measurements—height, weight, and head circumference. The doctor checked his reflexes and said that my son appeared to be hitting all the expected mental, emotional, and motor milestones. But.

But?

He had declined two percentile on the growth chart for his weight.

What?

The doctor explained, "On paper this is a textbook sign for failure to thrive, but by looking at your son, he seems to be thriving OK. He just needs to gain more weight. I recommend adding cereal to his diet."

I am the worst.

Somehow it never occurred to me that my precious baby wasn't gaining enough weight. I thought that I had all the right checklists, and I was following the ideal scheduling guidelines with feedings and naps and tummy time. I felt I had failed.

How could I have missed this?

I was visibly mortified. To encourage me, the doctor said, "You're a wonderful mom. I see a lot of parents in my clinic, and I can tell that you're doing a great job and your son is doing OK. You will figure this out."

The problem was that this news zapped any faith that I had in myself, so I didn't think I could actually figure this one out. I pleaded with the doctor for any parenting advice or food tricks to get my son to eat more. He just kept telling me that I'll figure it out. I felt so alone.

The taller my son grew, the more noticeable it was that he was a skinny boy. Ashamed, I didn't tell many people about the news from that day. I held the burden close and hoped my son would eventually even out with a high-calorie diet. I was silently dying on the inside from the constant pricking of the *I suck* mantra. It felt like torture waiting for things to turn around, not knowing when it would actually be better. Not knowing if I was ever doing enough. He inched his way toward a healthy weight and is doing great today, but the guilt still lingers.

And then a well-meaning friend asked me, "So now that your son is four months old, what are you going to do?"

Wasn't I doing what I was supposed to be doing? Isn't being a mom enough?

I knew what she meant. She wanted to know if I was going to go back to work. Her pointed, but innocent, question propelled me into a spiral of self-doubt and re-evaluation of all my life choices for the following year. I wrestled with the unsettling thought that *I wasn't doing enough* because I was just staying home with my baby.

Do people think I'm lazy? Should I be doing more? Am I meant to do more than care for this little guy?

Every time someone jokingly asked me while I chased after my toddler, "What do you do all day," my body tensed with shame. Instead of seeing their comment for what it was—a joke—I chase my toddler all day obviously, I assumed everyone was judging me, thinking I binge watch TV and snack on Milanos while fairies rub my feet and shower me with warm, fuzzy compliments. You could say that I was overly sensitive to the opinions of others—*Am I a subpar mom, am I doing enough, am I fitting into some cultural ideal?*

What kind of mom am I supposed to be?!

Looking back, I likely had undiagnosed postpartum depression—or an identity crisis. Maybe both.

I also had to learn to accept my new postpartum body with the saggy skin, stretch marks, and leaky boobs. I struggled with my identity while trying to figure out how to do this whole thing for the first time ever.

Motherhood is stressful in the twenty-first century with the pressure to "keep up with Instagram" while staying aware of current parenting matters and trends. I stressed over the harmful effects of screen time on brain development and social media bullying. I worried about the balance between offering my kids enough structure to thrive but also not over-scheduling their day so they could learn to cope with boredom. I Googled the effect of co-sleeping versus sleep training and found that they're both right for varying reasons. Who knew that secondary drowning was a thing in the '80s? Well, I knew about it as a twenty-first-century mother, and you better believe I was thinking about it every time my child was near water.

I could instantly find someone on the internet who was doing something better than me, and there were countless bullet-point lists of dos and don'ts for parents to follow. My barometer for measuring how much I suck moved with every swipe and click.

A picture of mom friends getting together to meal prep for the next month for their families. *Man, that sounds smart and fun. Why don't I plan ahead like that?*

Swipe.

Picture of a family with matching T-shirts for their kid's themed birthday party. *How did she have time to plan ahead so they could make their kid feel extra special with matching T-shirts that fit the themed party? They look so perfect. I can barely get the cake and presents together for my kids.*

Swipe.

A picture of a family taking their baby and toddler on their first camping trip. *How are they surviving? Even the amount of work it takes to pack for a trip, care for a child in the car, and then operate normal life outside of your familiar home is near insanity. But to do that in the wilderness? What do I not know? She must be a better mom than me.*

Unintentionally and intentionally comparing myself suffocated my soul and killed my contentment, peace, and joy. Plus, the math didn't add up. Reading what someone fed their kids for breakfast sucked more energy out of me than added to me, taking up brain space that I barely even had. Those darn five seconds put me on a negative trajectory. If this was a math problem, it would look like this:

Brain (1)—Useless Social Info (5) =-4

Take it one step further:

Brain (-4)—Staged Life Highlight photo of a Supermom (10) =-14

Comparison was an easy trap, and boy oh boy, it was a vicious beast that fed my shame, fear, and pride. Not worth it. My brain was tired anyway. My thoughts were incoherent. And my self-esteem plunging. The lie that I suck at keeping my life together kept forcing itself to the front of my mind. I knew something had to change if I was going to survive. No one can operate on negative energy and feel like they are thriving in life.

CHAPTER 3
I Live to Survive the Grind

And so it began. Like clockwork for years, my son would wake up every night at least once, if not twice or thrice for various reasons. Once his sister was born and nursing regularly, nighttime turned into a parade of zombie children with an occasional trick dog whenever she felt left out of the nightlife bustle. And without fail every morning, my son would wake up at five o'clock. Patiently standing by my bedside, his precious innocent breath would tickle my eyelashes awake, and as soon as our eyes met, we would embrace each other and talk about our sweet dreams. Oh, who am I kidding? My eyeballs popped open at the startling sound of the door opening, and his grand announcement that he was ready for breakfast. Being jerked awake like this every morning never helped me start the day well. Instead, it lurched me into instant stress, which I'm pretty sure, is against the doctor's orders. Now grumpy, I fought the inner turmoil of an ever-increasing sleep debt. I usually manifested stress physically, but my clenched jaw and white-knuckled fists took it to a new level. After a minute or so of listening to my inner dialogue whine, I could usually muster up enough willpower to do my mommy duties. I don't know why I acted so offended like my little innocent child knowingly robbed me of something—mainly my sanity. Thank the Lord they are cute. Why else would we allow another person to treat us like this?

And so every day began with a feeling of lack—loss. I'd get up and do what needed to be done. This was the job—only a season I'd tell myself. Like a manufacturing company, I created schedules and moved through the same motions every day. But eventually, I realized how quickly plans changed and shifted for moms in the tiny human world. If you're not flexible, well then have a baby. You figure out how to do metaphorical backbends all day long around public tantrums, poop on the hall floor, Sharpie stains on the couch, Legos up the nose, and spills, spills, spills! Over time, I learned how to absorb these unexpected situations like an extra-long maxi pad, the kind with the protective wings.

Of course, in between the schedules and the unanticipated moments, I sprinkled as much sound discipline and wisdom that I could throughout the day. I mean, the goal was to raise decent humans, right? But if I'm honest, my words probably sounded incoherent half the time, shrouded as they were in brain fog. It was hard enough to make a mental grocery list.

Ok, we need eggs, bread, and—

"Hey, Mom! Watch me jump." My daughter leaped straight up in the air with a satisfied grin on her face.

"Oh, wow! Good job, Honey." *OK, so that was eggs and br—*

"Hey, Mom! Watch this jump now." Excitedly, she waited for my attention and then jumped about a foot forward.

"Oh, wow! Honey, that's great. Mommy needs to make the grocery list now, OK?" Hoping she gets my hint.

"Hey, Mom! Can you see me do it again? Watch this time!" Proud of herself, she propelled herself forward another foot.

"You're so good at that! Now give Mommy five minutes without any interruptions, OK? I need to finish making the list before we go grocery shopping."

"OK!" And she happily waited . . . right next to me.

OK, what were the first two things I needed to get?

When I rarely experienced two consecutive thoughts together, how was I supposed to pull off heart-changing advice for my young impressionable children? With every interruption I sensed my brain growing wearier and my body tenser. I could feel all my jangled nerves; if someone looked at me the wrong way, I would likely burst into tears. You could say I was on edge. I craved quiet, thought-free moments, so I could simply remember how to breathe again. I found I was holding my breath like it was my sanity. My life had no exhale. This wasn't working and I didn't feel normal or healthy.

Then I saw it. A meme that had gone viral thanks to every parent everywhere. It pictured Théoden from *The Lord of the Rings* standing ready at Helm's Deep watching the nasty Uruk-hai beasts charge at him. His face looks tired and worn. His shoulders weighted by the anticipation of the inevitable onslaught roaring toward him. His eyes dark. And in bold white letters, it said, "You hear your children wake up in the morning . . . and so it begins." *Yes!* This was me! This is how I felt every day as I gathered myself to take on the onslaught of messes, nagging, and sibling rivalries.

I remembered the wise advice from my sister before I birthed my first child. She said, "It's all about survival in the beginning." *That's ominous*, I thought at the time. But she was right. So I set my sights on one thing— survival. Every day I was Théoden trying to survive every rush of exhaustion and frustration I felt trying to raise these tiny people.

In my mind, if Mommy was defeated, then the whole family suffered. The survival mindset was to protect the asset, me, and come to find out, anything chocolate seemed to do the trick. As soon as the precious eyelids of my babes were actually shutting for the night, I rewarded myself like a loyal golden retriever. I'd feed myself treats and shamelessly blast through episodes of *Gilmore Girls.* It was my guilty pleasure and it felt earned. These pleasures became my mechanisms for coping—surviving. I viewed motherhood much like a corporate job with very specific requirements but minus the W2. I saw it as a part of life, a system of things, and you just have to do it. I had pamphlets, email lists, and books available to keep me on track with milestones. Blogs were there to explain why my child decided to stop sleeping through the night at four months of age— answer, this is a common age for sleep regression. I had Pinterest to inspire potty training tricks. Instagram showed me creative snack ideas and fancy star-shaped sandwiches. Facebook was listening to me, so every advertisement was exactly what I needed. And Google turned me into a certified pediatrician or hypochondriac depending on how you looked at it. With checklists and information within "finger-clicking" reach, I had all the resources I needed to do my job.

This method of trying to keep things under control frequently felt out of control.

I felt stuck on a big hamster wheel trying to do my part while raising the next generation. My daily goal was to safely and responsibly raise my darling babies, so I could check out late at night with something chocolatey and cakey. And then after so many trips around the sun, my kids would eventually grow up and raise their own children and eat late-night snackies. And so the hamster wheel and binge eating would continue for generations to come. This was the point of existence?

Depressing.

I felt guilty for not understanding the honor in raising up the next generation just so the cycle could repeat. When does it stop and people start doing something more with their lives? And then I felt guilty for asking. But if raising the next generation looks like binging on chocolate and Netflix just to cope with the stresses of the day, then, truth be told, it's not as honorable as it's cracked up to be. Trust me, I loved indulging in *Gilmore Girls* a decade later than the rest of the world. It was comforting at the end of a long day. It was my "me" time. But these coping mechanisms were a temporary pleasure. I still felt stuck surviving life, and I was tired. So darn tired. Something had to change because deep down I knew this was not the life I was called to live—at least not like this.

Coping mechanisms are not all bad, especially if they make you a happier, healthier person. The two-hour childcare at the local gym proved to be pure gold. This was when I had my most meaningful, uninterrupted conversations with friends.

I had just finished a workout at the local YMCA when I grabbed a seat next to my dear friend and mentor, Kelly. We planned to grab a cup of free coffee at the gym cafe while we brilliantly utilized the second hour of our childcare limit. We lived for these moments. It seemed that we both just longed for these periods of freedom to "tap out" of motherhood even if the coffee was subpar. We laughed about how much joy we found in our mini mom-vacation.

I asked Kelly, "Why can't we sustain this same joy when we tap back into normal life?"

We agreed that it's a miserable existence to resist the majority of our day just to live for a handful of "free" hours. We both loved our lives and our babies, but something felt backwards relating to it all this way. It was an unpleasant way to exist.

I sat there thinking again about the pointlessness of an existence based on coping. What was I striving for? What was driving the need for my mom breaks? I knew exactly what I needed—grace and peace. Grace for myself and much more grace for my children. My heart, mind, and soul desired peace in the midst of the chaos. I realized then that these mom breaks allowed me to tap out and regain a sense of peace for myself before I jumped back into real-life duties. But it didn't matter how many breaks I got or how many girls' nights out I had, it never gave me lasting relief. Although I fully appreciated the breather, I desperately needed an enduring peace that could withstand a toddler tantrum the following day. I needed to be more emotionally equipped for my day-to-day grind. Anyone can learn how to tread water, but if you're going to cross the English Channel, you have to figure out how to swim well.

After talking with Kelly, I knew it wasn't just my own personality grinding against this survivalist existence, but it was all moms everywhere. Also, I had already taken every personality test available, and I discovered that no tests will tell you that you're a normal mom with a wonderfully created soul that's designed for an abundant life. Nope. The closest I got was probably the "What Disney Princess am I" quiz, but even still, the results were confusing. The truth that I had to realize was that we are not created to remain in a primal lifestyle of feeding and sleeping. We are complex creatures full of ideas, passions, and inspirations. Life is meant for living! I believe mothers should not be excluded from the abundant life just because they are busy nurturing tiny people. The more I thought about my current existence and the gut feeling that there is more to life, the more dissatisfied I became in letting life pass me by.

My survival mode was unraveling. My panties were literally in a wad from all the auto-response muscle clenching I did throughout the day. My darling nine-month-old had discovered that she gets immediate attention when she screams super loud. Butt clench. My precious four-year-old yelled, "I don't love you anymore!" and ran off to his room because he wasn't allowed candy for breakfast. Butt clench. I conceded that life was better without the panties. Checking out became an easy default to cope with all the stresses and muscle spasms. Plus, good underwear was expensive.

At this rate, I was running out of underwear, and commando wasn't an appealing option. Something had to change. Sheryl Sandberg challenged women to lean in. Likewise, I decided to stop surviving life and figured out how to thrive. I found a way to "tap in" while deep in the trenches of motherhood and stop depending so heavily on my brief moments of "tapping out." I was determined to live my life instead of being consumed by it.

CHAPTER 4
I Don't Have Time for Expensive Underwear

My best plan going forward was to scope out other moms who clearly walked around more comfortably than I did—figuratively picking at my twisted-up underwear. I struck gold when I befriended Kelly, the coordinator of the popular Mothers of Preschoolers local chapter. As a mother of three children, the last two being twins, she immediately called me out for comparing my handle on motherhood to hers. I guess I did idolize her a bit. On top of raising three children and leading a MOPS group of seventy-five women, she was a writer, owned a small business, had coherent, thoughtful conversations, memorized scriptures, and was living joyfully. She figured out how to have a life within motherhood! At the time, I had given up entirely on having a hobby, let alone a life!

When she invited me to Carla Maclachlan's discipleship class, I immediately said yes. I secretly just wanted to spend more time with Kelly, so I could learn her rhythm for life. Maybe her secret would rub off on me.

When I arrived at the first class, Kelly had already saved me a seat next to her. Relieved, I sat down in the chair and looked around the room full of people. Carla walked toward the front of the room, introduced herself, and immediately launched into the material. She began explaining that the core need for all human beings beyond food, water, and shelter is peace. We all need to feel OK. She began connecting our need for love and acceptance to peace, which takes a faith based in grace abounding through self-discipline. We talked about salvation, parenting, and living abundantly. Carla quoted Bible verse after Bible verse from memory, convinced that God has given us all things that pertain to living an abundant life.

As I was taking notes, Kelly leaned over and told me this was her fourth time taking the class, and I realized that this was the gateway to Kelly's world—discipleship. This was how she operated. The truths in this class formed the basis for her mindsets and approach to raising her babies.

Carla stopped and instructed everyone to underline **2 Peter 1:2–4** in their Bible, memorize it, and recall it in every circumstance. It says, "Grace and peace be multiplied to you in the knowledge of God and of Jesus our Lord, as his divine power has given to us all things that pertain to life and godliness, through the knowledge of him."

That's it. I thought. It's in the knowledge of God that grace and peace will abound. The answer is him! He has freely given me all things that pertain to life—that must include motherhood. I sat considering this verse as a truth that not even cultural progression, social development, or a new Baby Einstein product can undo. So *why don't I turn to him to find grace and peace? How do I turn to him when I feel like I'm drowning?* I craved a thriving life. Living for my mom breaks felt like a dead-end—going nowhere, stagnant. I knew that he promised to draw near to me if I draw near to him, so if this is a true A + B = C situation, I figured I could turn to him in the thick of the day and discover more peace, more grace, more wisdom, and a more abundant life. And, boy oh boy, I sure need the help! All I had to do was take the action step and create a new habit of turning to God—tapping into his grace and peace.

Each week in Carla's class, I scribbled notes about how I could create a more abundant life by tapping in instead of out. And each week, I became more dissatisfied with coasting through life, in comfort and stagnation. I was inspired to shift my mindset and commit to focusing on the source of grace and peace. Because of my change in perspective, the misconception that I didn't have enough time to change my life unraveled.

Admittedly, beginning the practice of changing my point of view with an exhausted zombie brain wasn't easy, but alternatively, tapping out wasn't producing much in me other than a sugar addiction. I recognized that I can only live today once, so I started making changes one day at a time learning how to tap in. I pressed into the wildness, turning toward it instead of away and I found grace along the journey.

CULTIVATE BELIEFS FOR TAPPING IN

CHAPTER 5
Monkeys and Coconuts

The reality was that I wasn't any better at dealing with life than a Southern Indian monkey with a handful of candy. I didn't make the connection right away, but there was an immediate primal bond when I heard this story in church one Sunday. It immediately hit home: Ah yes, I thought, **Psalm 46:11**, *"Be still and know that I am God."* A verse I knew well. I fully anticipated nodding my head through the sermon like the words were nothing more than a nice reminder of what I already knew. Self-righteous, I know. But then came the monkeys. The pastor described the trouble that monkeys were causing homes and businesses in India. It sounded awful. Monkeys were breaking into homes and wreaking havoc all throughout Southern India—shredding belongings, eating the food, pooping wherever, and stealing whatever they please.

The locals cleverly discovered a way to safely capture the monkeys as to not harm the sacred animal. They hollowed-out a coconut, tethered it to a stake, and stuffed it with something enticing like candy. The opening was strategically carved so the monkey could slide its open flat hand into the coconut but would not be able to pull his fist back out after grabbing the bait. What the monkey never realized was that it was possible to escape—he just needed to let go of the bait and slip his hand free. However, the unwavering desire to keep hold of the candy kept the monkey hostage. Holding onto the craving for, the lust for, the coveting of this thing—the bait—led to certain capture. But letting go of that "thing" led to freedom. The choice was always there.

The idea that monkeys would surrender their freedom for the sake of a piece of candy seemed ludicrous. Forgetting that this whole story was being told to me for a reason, I marveled at the foolishness of these animals. While I was lost imagining obsessive monkeys trapped by coconuts, the pastor explained that the literal Hebrew translation of "be still" is "to let go, to release, to surrender."

There it was.

In the original grammar of "be still and know that I am God," the emphasis is on the second imperative. Meaning, we must be still (let go, surrender) in order to know God—his power, strength, and sufficiency. The act of giving up trust in ourselves, in people, material things, ideas, and so on allows us to objectively experience the all-sustaining, all-powerful work of God. If I chose to let go of whatever held me back, I could find freedom, peace, rest, joy! I craved those things. If I just got out of my own way, I had space to invite God to work in my life. Or at least notice it.

My head was spinning. All I could think about were the hypothetical coconuts that I woke up with every morning when I begrudgingly chant "and so it begins . . .". I asked myself, what was I choosing to hold onto that held me back from a liberated life? I needed to figure it out. This, I felt, was the key to breaking through to abundant living while in the trenches of preschool schedules and potty training. First, I needed to understand that I had a choice. No one enticed me with coconut traps in the morning. I was not faultlessly grumpy. On my own, I had been choosing to give power to my selfishness, impatience, or frustration, acting on offenses like it was my job to bring justice to my life. Holding onto bitterness from comparing myself one too many times to the families that seemed better off, or happier, or more put together, or like they had parenthood figured out. This led to sourness and sadness in my own heart, and that's not fun for anyone to be around. The option to choose helped me look up from my hypothetical coconuts and realize that this wasn't the only way to live out my days—nor the best way. I didn't have to choose impatience or frustration. A lot of times the better choice was not easy. It took cultivating a life to support the person I wanted to be.

I don't know if my breakthrough was triggered by turning thirty, and suddenly not giving a crap about what others think, or if it was the realization that I was living a life on the brink of shattering. Living between the pull of loving the precious little years and needing some serious space was a tough paradigm. I hated losing my patience when my kids couldn't find their shoes when we needed to leave the house, like right now. I hated feeling frustrated when my kids would not eat their food. Every. Single. Meal. I hated that I oozed selfishness and took personal offense when my children fought bedtime and interrupted my "me time" every fifteen minutes until 11:00 p.m. I did not want to live this way. I thought that, surely, if I let go of the ugly ogre once it rises up in me, I'd be free. I fully believed Jesus's words to his disciples: "I have come so you might have life . . . more abundantly." I just didn't understand how it applied to motherhood. I knew it was true, and women are not exempt from that truth as soon as they pass a kid into the world. *It must be true for me too! Living abundantly.* Somehow I knew there was a way for every mother drowning in piles of laundry and the sounds of her whining children to live abundantly.

Sister, you are called to an abundant life. But hello! (Speaking to myself at the time), you must start living first! Yes, the fatigue is debilitating some days. But my goodness! You must know that you were not born to be a zombie going through the motions of playdates, naps and story hours. The abundant life is for you, and it starts by stopping, savoring, and letting go. Take a breath and exhale out all the pent up pain and frustration. Do it again. And again. Until you can finally feel yourself ease in to rest—that space where you no longer hold on but instead feel held. And remember that you matter. Yep, you're a mom, but you are also So. Much. More. You have talents and passions unique to you that are not meant to be squelched because your time is spent making monthly letter boards and organic baby food. God sees you, and it feels good to be noticed. He loves you in both your finest moment and in your messiest moment. Yeah girl, your postpartum rolls, stinky hair, and tired eyes are a masterpiece right now! He didn't create you, say that you were good, and then wipe his hands of you. You are still his great work today! You just have to see it and receive it. This is the bizarre thing to grasp; the thing to stop and ponder—unconditional love . . . A deeply rooted confidence that summits your soul when you know that you're loved. Personally, I'd rather my soul live in freedom of knowing I'm loved than wallowing in self-doubt and criticism that comes from comparing myself to the world.

So be still, let go, and know God. This is where the magic happens. Letting go naturally frees the heart to accept more peace, grace, and love. And out of that, the heart can come alive. Maybe God just wants us to trust him in the process of letting go and to fall into his embrace instead of getting caught up in the worry of what happens if we relinquish control.

This, my friends, is when I realized that I may need faith to wipe butts after all. This was no longer a job. I set off on a mission to rediscover life—mom style. The following chapters contain all the ways I found to let go and tap into a more fulfilling life.

CHAPTER 6
Stiff Arm like a Mother

So, how then?

My heart wanted to trust and let go, but I was physically too tired to convince myself that it would be OK. My brain didn't feel safe letting go. And I was still miserably controlling my messy sticky life and suffocating myself with this idea coconut that I wasn't doing enough as a mom. I strived to be better, always. I created a healthy snack tray, so I could ensure my kids developed healthy eating habits. I mapped out time for outside free play to foster their imaginations and develop creative problem-solving skills through the art of boredom. I limited screen time. I valued exercise. And then I would inevitably scroll past an article on social media telling me five things I was not doing that I should be doing with my toddlers, piling the weight of guilt onto my weary shoulders.

I wonder if this is one of those coconuts I could lay down?

Maybe, I thought, I could disregard it and just trust that I'm doing OK. So I swiped past it like I just stiff-armed the corner back of motherhood demons and ran for a touchdown. It was liberating.

I started there—letting go of societal pressures and advice that I didn't ask for from articles written by strangers that don't know me or my kids. This may seem like a basic place to start, but I felt like I embarked on the *mother loaded* secret.

I knew striving to be a great mom was good. I had figured out how to pick and choose what brought my family freedom. As I peeled back the scales covering my pride and ego, I could decipher what advice was healthy for our particular family. I worked on knowing what informed my decisions. *Am I going to this playdate because I like the other families or because I want to feel popular? Do I want to buy a BOB stroller because it's what I need or am I wanting to fit in with the moms that seem to have it all together? Do I really feel like love and logic is the only way to parent my children? Do I really think it's OK to wear yoga pants all day and not make any effort to look good?* With each question I asked myself, I came to know myself better. And it wasn't pretty. Intertwined with my goal to be a good mom was the silent goal to uphold an image. But the truth was that I was worn out. So I started letting go, with a stiff arm, of things that fed my ego and pride, allowing me to be true to me and my family. I released social pressures and norms. Pulling back allowed me space to evaluate what I truly felt was important in my life. I found that the impact of loosening my tight grip after being subconsciously spread so thin emotionally and mentally for such a long time is twofold. First, the air felt better to breathe. It was satiating and calming. So that was good. Secondly, I saw myself. I had to see myself and be present in my life. That was hard. I practiced settling in to who I was, remembering that I am me, and this is who I am here to be in this world. Understanding this is truly liberating.

Avoiding comparison on every platform and reeling my big Looney Tune eyes back into their sockets was a good start. Cutting the highlight reel of others and no longer comparing my daily grind to that, eventually led me to discover the grand life secret—that I was OK. I am fabulously not perfect. In fact, no one is. I was free to refocus my life, accept myself, and increase my survival rate in motherhood. This was imperative.

Through this, I discovered contentment in the present moment. When I stopped imagining what my life should look like and comparing it to others, I had a fighting chance to transform my personal happiness. So I stopped looking to the future or thinking about the past, and I learned the power in loving what is. I embraced today. I loved today. I accepted myself now. My translation: pure freaking bliss. This is contentment.

Contentment means peaceful happiness. We all want to be happy moms, so why wait? The idea that you'll be happier once your Instagram looks perfect, or when you lose the baby weight, or when the mom down the street invites you to her monthly girl's night is false. You probably know this. And the thought that you'll feel better once the kids finally sleep through the night or once you don't have to change diapers anymore is only partially true. Yes, there is a relief that comes, but without healthy habits and mindsets in place, the next stage of life will take you on another nose dive. Learning to stop focusing on the next thing that will make you happy—a milestone, weight loss, girls' night out—is hard, but achievable. Happiness is a byproduct of a change in perspective, but not the focus of the perspective. No one is exempt from unhappiness

Once I laid down my own measuring stick, I realized I did want more out of life—for myself this time. I was measuring me with me. Asking myself what kind of life I wanted, not what some internet list was telling me I needed to be. I needed to thrive. The last time I checked, I was breathing, so I deserved to feel alive, right? I needed answers. I wanted to feel better, stronger. It was hard enough to remember to make sure all my kids had shoes on before I left the house, so digging deeper to figure myself out was a big step.

CHAPTER 7
Be Unoffended

Raising little munchkins can definitely feel like a battle to make it to the end of the day. They are certainly not Uruk-hai beasts like I may have alluded to in chapter one. No, kids are preciously created individuals that need attention in differing ways that consume your life. The constant needs, interruptions, and unexpected snags in the routine raked at my inner peace while my heart melted at their adorableness. I was an exhausted mess, hitting the reboot button all day long. Plans and schedules remained in a constant pliable state in order to absorb unforeseen accidents, tantrums, or blowout diapers. Nothing prepared me for the day that I walked into the nursery to pick up my child after a nap only to discover that she had learned how to remove her diaper and paint herself, the crib, and the wall with poop. I didn't even know where to start reconciling this. *Clean baby first, just start there.* And I absorbed the fact that the afternoon plans may not happen, and I was instead going to remain cooped up in my house doing poop cleaning all afternoon.

In the chaotic, crazy-making moments, perspective was everything for my sanity. Stillness and letting go became my practice. In these less than glorious moments, I had to learn to find the glory of **Psalm 46:10**, "Be still and know that I am God". The grounding perspective that I could translate to weary child-rearing days was to not take every hiccup as a personal infringement on my plans, time, or capability to be a good mother.

I had to become unoffendable.

When my sweet pea put her yogurt snack all over her head and I had to commence a new afternoon plan on the spot, I learned to react in stillness and proceed with the understanding that she wasn't purposefully putting us behind an extra thirty minutes. She just wanted to experience the feeling of yogurt on her body.

When I was in a season of experimenting "what will my kid eat today," I had to find a way to approach each meal with an open heart, free of the expectations that would lead to frustration and impatience. The Lord may be the only one that really knows why my children love spaghetti one night and then despise it another night. When dinner surprises like this happened, I had to constantly let go and release feelings that would only produce more negativity in me.

All parents learn different techniques on how to roll with it when these things happen. But the rolling still left me breathless. Choosing to be unoffended gave me a sense of control when unpredictable events happened. It kept me steady while treading new courses of action.

Part of me thought, *Don't they know that we have schedules and appointment times that we need to honor? The world doesn't revolve around them. And don't they know how hard I work at preparing them food multiple times a day? They should be so grateful!* When I stopped to evaluate my emotions linked to the expectations I placed on my kids—the "they shoulds . . . "—I could see that my own driven nature was causing significant stress in me and probably my kids. I'm not saying a free-for-all parenting approach is the answer because I wholeheartedly believe kids thrive with boundaries and standards. But I had to reflect on how I approached my own standards within the operation of my home.

When I stopped taking offense to the actions of my kids and realized they're not personally attacking me, I could more clearly evaluate what was going on in my own heart. When my son flicked on the bedroom light at 5:00 a.m., he was excited for the day and not purposely startling me awake as a prank. So I let go of the offense. When my kids interrupted me multiple times, it was clear that they had not learned their manners well enough, and I needed to teach this social skill more effectively. Again, the offense fell to the wayside. Innocence does not warrant taking offense. As a result of releasing offenses, it allowed space for grace in my heart and space for breath. Taking the focus off myself and my personal expectations, I could be less reactive and more gracious.

CHAPTER 8
Fracking Feel Better Method

Letting go of societal pressures, personal offenses, and comparisons, I felt like I was in a constant Donkey Kong mode trying to dispose of any bad karma coconuts corrupting my chances for winning at peace and grace. Although it made me feel better, I still didn't feel like I was winning. Acknowledging my flaws was a nice step forward, but it didn't teach me how to make a lasting difference. Then I remembered **2 Peter 1:2-4**, "Grace and peace be multiplied to you in the knowledge of God and of Jesus our Lord, as his divine power has given to us all things that pertain to life and godliness, through the knowledge of him." Recalling everything from the class with my mentors, Carla and Kelly, the answer came crashing in like a wave. It's in the knowledge of God that grace and peace increase! So, I need to know God. But where do I start? I went back to **Psalm 46:10**, "be still [let go] and know that I am God."

That's it.

I missed the stillness part— the stopping, the pause. I had to understand that letting go was not a drive-through action step. It must be savored.

Over time, I learned that pausing was a practice and essential to begin releasing anything. In these moments, my body had the opportunity to grasp the present. I found gratitude in what was good around me. I set my mind and heart on something beyond myself to teach me how to find peace and grace and ultimately-contentment.

Contentment is a mindset. It starts with stopping. Within that place, we can learn to let go and lean into God. But the truth is as a mom, we don't even have time to savor a hot cup of coffee unless the stars align and the sun and moon collide. So I say, frack this life.

Seriously. Stay with me.

Fracking is the geological term for the process of injecting liquid at high pressure into subterranean rocks so as to force open existing fissures and extract oil or gas. When oil companies need oil, they don't sit around for the right moment. They make it happen. Yes, I'm using this oil industry term as a life hack metaphor, but we can use the same principles in motherhood. Again, stay with me. Try injecting, with purpose, micro-moments in your day that produce the thing that you're after—grace, peace, knowing God. The discipline of making a change is the key. Insert moments to practice pausing, letting go, and savoring what is good and constant while deep in the grind of raising little ones. These micro instances will add up throughout the day, and if done in creative ways will prove that this practice is fantastically not limited by time.

This should be encouraging!

Five-second blips count. Blip fracking is truly effective! As a busy mom, I never spent hours meditating to center myself. I had to cultivate a mindset within the hustle, embracing the daily routine but approaching it differently. These little blips built a foundation that kept me connected to a calming constant, and the more I leaned into it, the more peace, rest, and strength I felt. In this ever-changing world of raising babies, that constant kept me steady. Some could interpret the constant as your own soul or the earth or the presence of God. I personally leaned on God. Scriptures say he is never changing (**Hebrews 13:8**) and that steadiness comforted me. Savoring him in a moment of stillness or a five-second blip between baby squeals and toddler questions will, in fact, produce contentment. It's a sense that you are OK, life is OK. Where you are is OK. In fact, it's good. It's from this place, this mindset, this pausing, that the abundant life can flow.

Doing this may seem overwhelming. If so, start with inserting more truth in your life. Surround yourself with scripture or quotes that you want to learn to live by. Invest in a chalkboard, so as the seasons change in your life, you can update the words on the board that you want to impact your life. Hang it in a place that you can see frequently, reminding you to savor what it says. It needs to be noticeable. The goal is to surround yourself with ideas that lift you up and encourage you to press forward to the joy you desire to have in your life.

Another idea would be to grab an inspirational calendar. They are available in flip charts or books. Find one that speaks to your soul. Put it on your nightstand, and read it before bed or right when you wake up. Put it in the bathroom and read it while you get ready in the morning. Try not to get stuck on the idea that you need to read a million books to be moving forward in your personal growth. I had to stop getting caught up in the quantity of time I spent reading and refocus on the quality of what I was reading in the little time I had. Due to lack of sleep, my brain could only manage a small amount of deep thinking before it got all mushy anyway. So micro hacks were just perfect. Over time these moments will morph into an abiding lifestyle.

Psalms 91:1 says, "Whoever dwells in the shelter of the most high will rest in the shadow of the almighty." Are you laughing? I'm sure your tired eyes are just having a hard time getting through this page, so the idea of getting some rest sounds pretty absurd, right? It was a different kind of rest than we're physically used to. Just like that feeling of comfort and security. That feeling of calm inside of your heart where you can exhale without fear of the future. It's the type of rest where you don't have to worry about who you are because you are fully known and fully loved.

It's like that same feeling of when you first fall in love, and you feel like you could do anything in the world. It's exciting and thrilling. You can blast through the day with incredible energy because your heart is ignited and beating out of your chest. Your soul exudes an unexplainable courage and confidence powered by this tremendous knowledge of being loved.

The secret? Frack it and hack it. This discipline will transform your world.

CHAPTER 9
Snack-Making Warrior

Prayer is a pause. Naturally fitting my practice of stillness, prayer became a continual action step necessary for inviting faith into my mundane daily grind. The power came in shifting my focus from myself to the world around me and toward my creator. It helped me feel present when my brain fog was heavy and made it hard to function. It opened up micro spaces in the day to be still and really notice God. And within these brief moments, I held onto the truth that "every good and perfect gift comes from above (**James 1:17**)."

Life shifted when I chose to set my heart on finding the gift, the good thing, within moments. My days began differently. I could see the blessing of a new morning when my kids woke me up before the rising sun. Sometimes the mornings were pure wildness, and the good thing I focused on wasn't anything more profound than being grateful for the ability to breathe in oxygen. On easier days, sometimes the blessing was the sweet snuggles from my children, the brisk air of the promised new season arriving, the sweet conversations during breakfast, or the fullest joy the kids expressed for building forts with pillows and blankets. For all of this, I am thankful. This perspective was the breakthrough that helped me release my grumpy monkey tendencies and love my life!

As I extended this practice into more pockets of my day, the more waves of joy I experienced. Stopping to notice God's sovereignty while playing in the yard with my kids, I could truly appreciate the complexity of a flower and how it blooms in its right timing. I found awe in watching the bees retrieve what they needed from this flower because all was provided for the plant to prosper. This is something to be grasped. Taking time to realize this small yet meaningful interaction between the flower and bee and how significant it is that each has been uniquely provided for is a comforting thought. I'd like to believe that if this small flower has what it needs, then I, as a wonderfully complex human being, would have my needs (like more patience and grace) met in order to thrive. And in the wildness of raising small curious children, I found even more comfort in the faithful order of nature around me. Seeing that there is a structure to life outside of my messy home and it is keeping a healthy rhythm and balance to the world made me feel like maybe my life would soon stop unraveling. Somehow I felt that all would be ok and life will carry on as it should. This practice of pausing to notice these little things gave me a feeling of strength and steadiness—peace. Prayer became an active way of responding to these micro-moments. It captured the profoundness of a thought within those few seconds before it slipped away into blurry Neverland, or wherever that swirly place is that processes the sounds of toddlers whining and complaining. Prayer became my sacred stamp that I imprinted my day with, so at the end of the day, I could look back and remember the gifts that I experienced. Remembering the big, small, loud, and quiet acts of my ever-present, never-changing God while actively noticing him in life produced a heart full of gratitude which naturally allowed for a constant sense of peace. And this was what I longed for—peace.

When I pressed in to experience this peace through the practice of pausing, I found that my heart could more easily settle on the truths of God. Yes, in my mind I knew that God is gracious and loving and all-knowing. But when I took a second to stamp a moment into my soul through prayer, attributes of God transferred from just head-space understanding to a knowing that resonated deep in my heart. Suddenly the reminder list of God's attributes stuck on my fridge were no longer flyby words. They were weightier. They radiated off the page and connected with something deeper inside of me. Prayer, pausing to notice and respond, made this possible. It brought life to otherwise nonsensical and normal things in my day, like my ability to breathe, running water, food for the day, a loving friend, the warmth of the sun.

After praying and pausing, choose to be consciously aware of more as you go about your day—an encouraging stranger at the store, a cool breeze at the park, flowers blooming in the garden, giggles from the kids. These things can be easily seen and dismissed. But the act of gratitude will make you feel more alive in the moment. At the end of the day, it will fill your heart with contentment that you lived. No more going through the motions. No more racing past moments and beating the hours to get to bedtime. You will feel alive when you're present.

Out of the overflow of this practice, I learned to pray for my kids and family. The mundane tasks became my war maps. Dishwashing—my post to pray for the health of my family. Vacuuming—the time to pray for the friendships my kids will have and the life troubles they will face. Laundry—my spot to pray for the character of my kids and the wellbeing of my family. Snack making was a battlefield, and I was a warrior. Cleaning up messes had a deeper purpose. I wasn't perfect at this. But I did my best to set up habits in my home such that I was a mother of action and purpose, and not a mother of reaction floating through each day.

The spoken word contains so much power—giving life or death (**Prov. 18:21**). With that in mind, maintaining a healthy diet of affirmations provides powerful sustenance for a warrior mama. Beyond your thoughtful prayers for others, check in with your inner dialogue. Would you speak to your friends like that? We are all harder on ourselves than anyone else, so I'm asking you to evaluate the truths that you're telling yourself. We can't continue to build up those around us when we don't affirm ourselves. We will crash and burn.

Write down scripture that speaks of who you are or inspirational words that spark your soul. Put them wherever you need to hear it. Speak it over yourself every day. You are more than a booger wiper.

Focusing your mind on gratitude and a higher power may be hard when your kids are whining at you constantly. In these moments, I try to invite my children into the conversation, the noticing and pausing. This keeps me from becoming derailed, and it teaches my children how to have the same perspective as well.

With your children, start by noticing creation. See how the flowers lift their petals up toward the sun and are grateful for this miracle. Then ask them how God may be providing for your family just like he meets the needs of this flower with the sunlight. Consider how the body is designed for food, drink, and sleep. Help your children find gratitude for these things.

This act of giving thanks will shift the atmosphere and attitudes within your home. It's not a rose-colored glasses approach to life. It's a small change in perspective that transforms your life.

CHAPTER 10

Chicken Nugget Anytime Friends

I remember standing in my kitchen listening to my sweet dad express his frustration about how I never answer his phone calls anymore. Making mental notes, I remembered that I also had a couple text messages to return from friends as well. I was just behind—like always. The truth was I wanted to be better and more attentive to others, but raising babies pushed my personal margin so far that it left little room for much else. I felt misunderstood—mostly by people that weren't raising small children.

Within my mom circle, we upheld the understanding that response time is not a measure for friendship. Like some kind of unwritten code, we just knew that we would message each other when we remembered, which could mean next week. We realized that most likely the person saw the text but immediately got distracted by a crying baby or a toddler spilling cereal everywhere or by that heart-sinking silence that means your children are up to no good. We understood that you would love nothing more than to connect with your friends, but current circumstances are far more urgent.

These are the same people that would call me and ask if they could bring their kids over to hang out just because they needed to get out of their own house. They would bring the chicken nuggets and I would provide the Mac'n Cheese. As easy as that, we met each other with what we had, providing the right amount of relief and comfort that we needed to get through the day. Nothing about this was glamorous or Pinterest perfect. In fact, I likely had dishes in my sink and clean laundry that needed to be put away. This was real life. And it was perfectly wild and wonderful.

The time spent walking out normal life with a friend was so refreshing and encouraging for my soul. I felt less alone. And more often than not, I gained some sort of insight or mom hack just by being around them. I'm a better mom because I showed up for a friend as I am and with what I had. Nothing more.

These are the people to latch onto. The moms that understand the hardships you are facing. The women who can encourage you because they have been in your shoes before. The friends that can meet you as they are, not when they feel perfectly ready. The ones that offer chicken nuggets and grapes because it's what they have until grocery day.

Realizing the impact of positive friendships coupled with the power of perspective and prayer in my personal life, I organized a weekly prayer group of women focused on building each other up through prayer and friendship. We met between naptimes and school pickups. It was efficient for the sake of our schedules, but we stayed dedicated for the sake of our souls. We committed to calling each other during the week when the days became too much for our patience and we needed on-the-spot prayer. These women became my anytime friends. Anytime we would send messages of encouragement or prayers as we felt led to do so. We were on a mission to strengthen and comfort one another through connection and truth. We empowered one another. Moms gladly going to prayer on behalf of each other was the heart of the sweetest sisterhood of anytime friends.

CHAPTER 11
The Power in the Mess

Do the things taking up your brain space align with what you value? Are you focused on what matters to you or the world outside of yours? Remember that everyone is messy, but their mess may look different than yours. You need to ask yourself—what is important to you? Focus on that. If it's important for you to make sure your kids spend at least one hour outside per day, then you need to focus and make sure your schedule allows for that. Maybe you work full time in order to provide food and shelter for your kids or because you love what you do or so you can have enough money to travel the world. Everyone has the same twenty-four hours in one day, and the way you break down those hours will be unique to you and your family. So it's frivolous to compare your life to anyone else's. It's a waste of time to get distracted with envy. Time is precious right now, mamas. The good news is, whether you're a stay-at-home mom or not, your kids will grow up just fine! That's the goal, right? There is no one right way to do motherhood.

So the pressure to do what is "right" is off your shoulders. God is not judging you because you chose to sleep in a little extra this morning while your darling child watched Mickey Mouse Clubhouse. The beauty is letting go of our guilt to allow us to open our arms up to grace and receive it. Stop apologizing for the messiness of figuring out how to do motherhood. It's tough to receive grace when you are telling yourself you don't deserve it or you didn't do a good enough job to earn it.

Your focus and perspective are key to having confidence in life and the daily grind. Right now, remind yourself that you're not perfect, everyone is messy, and God's grace is sufficient for you. You are fully loved and accepted right now. You may have severe brain fog and coffee breath, but you are delightful to the Lord. Just as the blind man in **Mark 10:46–52** had nothing to offer Jesus, but simply desired something better—to see. And Jesus showed compassion toward him, and he was healed without needing to give anything in return. Likewise, just be, sister. Rest in the knowledge that whatever condition/status/shape you are in, God still loves you the same! It never shifts based on how well or poorly you behave as a mother. He loves you in this season.

"But in anonymous seasons we must hold tightly to the truth that no doubt strengthened Jesus throughout his hidden years: Father God is neither care-less nor cause-less with how he spends our lives. When he calls a soul simultaneously to greatness and obscurity, the fruit—if we wait for it—can change the world." Alicia Britt Chole, *Anonymous: Jesus' hidden years . . . and yours.*

Everything has its seasons—fashion, weather, plants, and you. You may not believe it, but this moment was made for you. Let me be clear. I did not say that you were made for this moment. In fact, I'm pretty sure nothing can fully prepare you for the surprises of motherhood. But this season of drinking cold coffee, consoling crying babies, and taking twenty minutes to convince tiny people to put their shoes on may seem like pure lunacy. And you may feel an ever-growing sense of isolation as you spend all day wiping up spills and dishing out snacks to thankless humans. It's hard to appreciate this time and stay encouraged when you get zero affirmation from the people you are working so hard for. But let me just tell you, it has its purpose. This time is for you—if you let it be.

Motherhood is the most refining relationship I know of; it's constantly pruning my character through life circumstances and calling me to dig deeper. Alicia Britt Chole describes it best in her book *Anonymous* when she recalls the life cycle of a tree. If a tree did not have the opportunity to shed its leaves, winter would kill the tree. Because of its bareness, it can enter a season of anonymity and brave the cold and dodge the weight of the snow. And like the tree, maybe the pruning has purpose in this season of your life. In her book, she reflects on the decades of Christ's life prior to his three years of ministry, recounting how vital those anonymous years were for him. Those years prepared him for the forty-day fast, temptations in the desert, the weariness of ministry, the dynamics within the twelve disciples, and the cross.

Likewise, motherhood can feel very anonymous even in our social media-driven world. Finding a sense of grandeur in tummy time and sensory play takes some stretching. Yes, we are raising the next generation, and that's not a small task. But that doesn't negate the feeling of anonymity that makes the job feel small because it doesn't reach outside the four walls of our home.

It can get lonely.

Pruning back our self-serving character traits, our priorities, and hobbies in order to serve someone who can't even speak the words, "thank you" doesn't happen without a level of pain.

Letting go and surrendering becomes a daily practice. But like the tree, this process is necessary for our ability to thrive. Alicia writes, "God is not a causeless God." This truth anchors an ever-changing life because it connects purpose to the coming and going, the hustle and the slowing.

The anonymous season of motherhood is mutually wild and sluggish. Someone has probably told you the days are long but the years are short. Well, that's the truth of the messy conundrum—it is, as the podcast title suggests, *The Longest Shortest Time*. The problem is that in the mess we can easily believe that the routine of naps, laundry, and washing bottles is our disappointing existence. Yes, everything you do is necessary for caring for your baby, and that alone matters one hundred percent! But it doesn't define you. It will, however, transform you if you embrace this anonymous season with its ebbs and flows.

I encourage you to see this less than glorious time full of potential purpose for your personal growth. Start shedding, letting go of the coconuts. Begin fracking your life with pauses and prayer. Create lifelong bonds in the ordinary with anytime friends. Embrace today. Love who you are now. Trust that God's love for you does not change based on how you feel. And remember the abundant life is for you too.

SECTION 3
PRACTICAL METHODS FOR TAPPING IN

CHAPTER 12
Take Charge

As a mom, we are always on alert. Constantly preparing to save the day, we operate mostly out of exhaustion and high anxiety. This effects our adrenal glands, our relationships, our sanity, and our health. Implementing the "be still" part of **Psalms 46:10** may seem darn near impossible in this state of surviving. We think—*We can't chill out. We can't let our guard down. Tiny people depend on us. And they are too loud and needy for me to have peace right now.* However, I promise you that your peace does not depend on your littles being peaceful. The stillness and calming is an internal practice—a perspective. It has to be, or we are all doomed for the next eighteen years.

Before we jump into practical ways to help you lift yourself out of survival mode, you need to figure out what you want. Take a second and consider what is important to you and what are your values. What brings you joy in life? Do you even remember? You may be so far gone that you've forgotten what hobbies are and what fun is. But I'm asking you to dig deep inside and make a list of things that bring you joy and that you value. See if those things could possibly lineup. Could you possibly coincide the things that are most important to you with something that brings you joy? Don't overthink it. It may be good to just start with the little things. Notice if having fresh flowers in your home gives you that extra burst of joy. Then buy some freaking fresh flowers and put them in your house. Or maybe working outside of your home is life-giving to you, and you thrive off of taking care of projects or managing people or running a business. It will be good to keep these things about you in mind as we walk through some implementations in the following chapters.

Fresh perspective and better focus is motivating for change. Practically speaking, I want to offer some tips to frack your life with. These life practices will help equip you as a mother to tap into the art of thriving. Girl, you got this. It literally comes down to a choice. Are you going to succumb to the suck, or are you going to figure out how to live better? I encourage you to choose to be brave and have faith during the hard days by choosing the thing that may seem inconvenient at the time knowing that what comes from it will be far better.

CHAPTER 13

Train Your Brain

TELL YOUR BRAIN WHAT TO THINK

There is so much power in our words. We can literally destroy ourselves, our mindsets, our perspectives—the things that shift attitudes and the environment in the home. Understanding this one thing is so important. That's why we should start with affirmations. What are you telling yourself every day? In the movie *School of Rock*, Joan Cusack, an uptight school principal, and Jack Black, the fun new music teacher, share a moment in a van where Joan confesses to Jack that she used to be cool. I often think about that moment in the movie while I'm wearing a headband and stained sweat pants, driving my minivan with my messy kids in their Cheerio-covered car seats. *Yeah, I used to be cool.* Even thinking this makes me feel sad. However, I'm pretty sure you wouldn't tell your friend that she is nothing but an overweight loser. So why would you tell yourself that? Be kind. The voice in your head is the only one that will be with you every second of your life.

To start, take a day or two to notice what you notice. How is your inner dialogue affecting the way you feel?

Do you feel bogged down by the pile of dishes in your sink? Do you feel guilty because you're rushed most days and rarely able to enjoy the present moment with your littles? Do you feel like you're making less of a contribution to the world because you're forgetting things constantly and losing your knack for intelligent conversations? Are you often having negative thoughts that pull you down? One thought can steer the way you experience a whole day. For instance, if I'm muffin topping my jeans, I would believe that I am just gross and incapable of maintaining a healthy lifestyle. My self-esteem tanks. This is the dumb truth: this one belief produces self-induced shame and ridicule that tears me down all day long. But I would never think this way about anyone else! I know I'm not alone in this. So, why do we allow these dumb thoughts to have so much power over us?

Imagine your best friend standing in front of you. Would you make her feel guilty for not keeping her house perfectly clean or would you shame her for not spending enough one-on-one time with her kids? Be honest. You would never say such things to someone that you loved. Girl, we need to evaluate the "truths" that we are telling ourselves. It's time to break the mean streak and treat ourselves like a decent human being.

So let's begin with this. Write down all the negative things you tell yourself. Close your eyes and imagine you are a friend talking to you. As a friend, what do you want to tell the real you? What do you need to hear knowing that she (you) is thinking all these horrible things about herself? Do you believe in her? Do you love her? Tell her exactly what she needs to hear right now. And then look at yourself in the mirror and tell yourself that exact thing. Notice how it makes you feel to talk to yourself this way instead of drowning in a cesspool of crappy thoughts.

You see, we all do this. We all speak the worst things imaginable to ourselves that we wouldn't even dare say to someone else. So why not do the flip side of that? Start speaking positive things to yourself that you would say to the people you love!

The Bible talks about how our words give life and death. And it says a good word is health to the bones. I know that I want health. It comes down to a choice. Studies have been done about speaking self-affirmations and how transformative it is to say the words out loud even when you don't believe it. That's because words are powerful. Start writing down three self-affirmations every morning. See what happens after a week and then a couple of months. Notice how it changes your thoughts; how it changes your attitude, your perspective. Notice your posture becoming taller and more confident. There is a boldness and bravery that comes when you believe in who you are.

That's where it starts—who do you believe that you are? Just a mom? You are more than that. You are a uniquely complex beautiful human being with gifts and talents that has the incredible job of raising children. You have so much to offer your family and this world. Your job is to honor what makes you unmistakably you while you raise the next generation. You are not created to toss your talents aside and lose yourself to the point of never finding it again. You have to start helping yourself believe in who you are even if you don't feel like it. So write down some affirmations. Post those words. Paint those words. Frame those words. Chant those words in the shower. Do this until you are convinced in your heart and in your mind of their truth.

On a side note, remember the voice your kids grow up hearing often turns into their own inner monologues. Speak life-giving words to your kids. He may be wrestling you and wiggling like crazy, making it nearly impossible to put a diaper on him, but you can tell him, "Wow, you are so strong; you are going to be stronger than your daddy one day", or "Your legs are moving lots so you must be a good runner. You're going to run fast one day."

Instead of speaking frustrations, speak life.

Now, look at your negative word list again. How true are they? Scratch through the exaggerations on the list and then pair down the raw truth. Is there a common motive or emotion tying any of them together? Work backwards on your truths. Could there be a deeper source to the impatience, short temper, or disconnectedness? For me, I needed to implement healthier habits like clean eating and exercise because if I didn't, it directly affected my attitude. For the sake of my sanity and the livelihood of my children, I had to make the change.

Next, ask yourself, how do you want to feel? Where do you want your focus to be? What is truly important today? This is the basis for your "why" in your change—the anchor to your breakthrough. What was important to me was a happier, healthier, thriving life with my children. And it all started with a renewed mindset.

"Fix your thoughts on what is true, and honorable, and right, and pure, and lovely, and admirable. Think about things that are excellent and worthy of praise" (**Philippians 4:8**).

The Bible talks about renewing the mind and setting your thoughts upon better things. This isn't just religious mumbo jumbo. Plenty of studies have been done on the power of thoughts and words. One Google search will prove that. Gratitude actually changes how our brains are wired. Scientists have found that maintaining a grateful mindset is one of the most effective ways to increase happiness. The more that you notice, the more you will notice. Count all the small blessings along with the big ones. It's the small gratitudes that build a practice of "seeing" daily that will anchor you during the tough days.

For me, putting some basic truths on the table—or the floor because that's usually where things end up anyway—I could stand on facts and not lies. You can begin here too. First off, double-check that your kid is alive. Yes? Great. You've managed to figure out how to keep a tiny helpless human alive. If your kid is as fearless as my daughter, who attempted backflips out of my arms every time I held her, you know how incredible this feat is. Next, check if you have had any food today. Yes? Great! You're managing to keep yourself fed while raising those munchkins! So, we've got the essentials covered. Anything beyond these are personal triumphs to be fully celebrated!

Did you make it to the grocery store and manage to get everything on your list? Maybe or maybe not. Maybe you did, but one kid threw a loud tantrum because you said he couldn't lick the cart and the other kid had a blow out diaper, resulting in you abandoning your full cart and racing to the nearest bathroom with a pungent stench following you. The point is—you did it. You cannot expect life to be flawless, so embrace the flaws. And no matter how messy things get, keep your eyes open to your triumphs—no matter how big or small. Every victory counts. You peed alone? That's a win. You slept for four hours straight? Win. You got to hire a babysitter and go out with friends? Another win. Keeping your eyes on the victories will prevent your mindset from shifting away from what is good and positive. It takes practice, but you'll soon realize you're already rockin' this. But if you can keep your thoughts on the successes and not the mess that ensued while achieving it, you will start realizing that you actually got this whole thing.

MAKE YOUR BED

Maybe you already do this. But for some of us making our bed is the last thing on our mind when we get woken up at five o'clock by our sweet little one. Or maybe we make our bed and like clockwork, it's a mess again by ten o'clock in the morning because of a daily dance party that happens in your room. The point is to find something that you can control. Something that you can do for yourself that gives you a sense of order in the chaos. Being able to walk in your room and see that your bed has been made will give you that sense of having something together when everything else seems to be a mess. I call it productivity wellness. At least you've completed this one thing you could tell yourself. If the whole day has been a mess and you didn't get one thing done on your to-do list, at least at the end of the day you can look at your bed and say I did that one thing.

Jordan Peterson has a fascinating perspective on life and the rules to live by. He suggests cleaning your room. Life is chaotic and cleaning your room ultimately gives you that sense of accomplishment and control that you can move forward from. Because if you are making decisions to bring order to things beyond your home but the place that you're making those decisions from is in chaos, then you're going to have a hard time keeping the order in the things that are outside of your home. So reel things back in. Find something in your home to have in consistent order. Maybe your kitchen counters are always clean. Or maybe your laundry is in order. When you're in a season of counting the small blessings, making your bed can have a greater impact and sense of accomplishment then you may think. Just find your thing.

GIVE ME FIVE

With a steady practice of seeing the good, the chaotic moments will have less impact on your emotions because you already have peace in your heart. A great way to fully cultivate this practice is by allowing your heart to experience life through all five senses. For instance, while changing the diaper of your wiggly four-month-old, take a second to really notice everything precious about that routine task. In doing so, the mundanity gains significance and depth. Notice the softness of his squishy legs, the smell of a clean diaper, the sweet giggles from a few tickles, the tiny fingers wrapped around your thumb, and the feeling of a gentle kiss on his nose. It's harder if you have multiple children. Just remember all it takes is an accumulation of fracking blips. Maybe make the effort to find one or two things to absorb about the moment. The goal is to be present and appreciate what is at that moment. And maybe part of that is enjoying the sound of your toddler's sweet high-pitched voice and the sight of his adorable waddle as he comes up and tugs on your side innocently seeking your attention.

It can be thoroughly consuming to be so present for everyone in our life. So start using all five senses to help you stay grounded in the moment because not being present would lead to a miserable existence. I believe most people don't realize how strong they really are. It takes adversity to call us to greater strength. Just like any strength-building fitness class, you have to break down the muscle to start making that muscle stronger. Likewise, the demands of motherhood have the power to make women stronger, wiser, kinder, and more compassionate. On the flip side, it also has the power to turn us into impatient grouches. It just depends on your perspective, values, and action steps.

GRATITUDE

One way to be more present and get a new perspective is to practice gratitude. Gratitude is a transformational practice that shifts your focus from the stress of life and draws out the hidden beauty in the mess. Start with a simple gratitude journal. This practice is guaranteed to produce more joy in your life. Embrace it. Your heart will feel the impact. There is power in gratitude. Start with a list of three things that you're grateful for and let it grow from there.

Do this along with your children. I personally started this when my son was four years old. Every day after school I'd ask him how class went. His response was always—bad. I asked him to tell me about his day. What

I figured out was that he fixated on one bad moment and decided the whole day was terrible even though there were actually a lot of wonderful things that happened too. Like so many adults, he chose to focus on the tough moment and let it ruin his whole day, even though he had way more good things happen to him. In order to break this pattern of thinking, we would spend five minutes before bed reflecting on the past twenty-four hours and listing as many things that we could think of to be thankful for. Now he can remember the day as a good one.

As mothers deep in the trenches of the diapers and toddler tantrums, we must remember the good! Journaling does not need to be organized, thoughtful, or in a specific setting. Put a small notepad in your purse so you can jot down some thoughts while waiting in the grocery check out. Put one by the coffee maker and write while the coffee brews. Put a journal on your nightstand or heck, on the back of the toilet! You get the idea. You have moments, though brief, where you can pause and reflect. It's an incredible way to reset your heart and find joy in the wildness of life. Practicing awareness throughout the day causes us to be present and grounded. Initially noticing the blessings with a grateful heart will keep your focus upward, so you don't drown amidst the storms of life.

On the contrary, if we keep our head down too long going through the motions of our schedules and checklists, we easily slip into a lifestyle that no longer notices and appreciates the greatness around us. We start living to catch our next breath.

For a short period of my life, I lived in one of the most beautiful places on earth—Colorado Springs. The city is nestled at the base of the massive mountain called Pikes Peak. Every day, I woke up to the grandeur. Its magnificence glowed in a fresh way depending on the angle of the sunlight, the number of clouds in the sky and my viewing point. The mountain felt wild and untamed, but also comforting. It was both welcoming yet daunting. We encountered rattlesnakes and bears, falling rocks and avalanches, but we always felt the beauty.

This awe of Pikes Peak lasted a while when I first moved there, but as my schedule became packed with play dates, school activities, and music lessons, I looked up less and less. Because I was distracted by life, the magnificent Pikes Peak no longer impacted me as much. Now if I can gradually stop noticing a massive mountain, then you had better believe I can gradually stop noticing a lot more than that.

I had to remember to pause and look up.

Awareness brings life back to the mind, body, and soul. Intentionally practicing gratitude, even in micro-moments, offers our humanness a chance to feel alive and less on an industrial line that's sifting to each new activity. I encourage you to be purposeful with your perspectives and awareness so you don't lose sight of the good things in life and end up consumed by the stresses instead.

MY BRAIN FROM OUTER SPACE

Truth be told, changing my perspective was transformational, but physically, I still felt like I was walking through mud every day. My fatigue crippled me. My nerves stood on end. I started having panic attacks. I often wondered, *Why can't I handle my life? I have a great life.* My perfect little life stressed me out, and I had no idea why.

I started searching for breakthroughs by getting a handle on my health. I bought vitamins, supplements, and a happy light. I joined a clean-eating challenge, removed chemical cleaners, and all things toxic from my house. I even diffused an essential oil named JOY. Gradually, life was improving. However, it wasn't until I dabbled in space technologies that I found my big ah-ha moment.

I thought I was simply establishing care with a new chiropractor and going through the usual assessments when I met Dr. Black. And then she asked me to put my finger on a scanner for five minutes. *Don't you want to ask me about my chronic neck pain?* She explained that this InsightTM Subluxation Station is certified space technology capable of determining my body's overall ability to adapt to stress; assess the balance and tone of my nervous system; measure my paraspinal muscle function, activity, and energy expenditure; and review the autonomic nervous system. *Um, what?* After that, she positioned another scanner on my C1 and C2 vertebrae and slowly moved it down my spine. She explained how important it is for the spinal cord to not be inhibited by incorrect alignment. Correct alignment allows the nervous system better and faster communication with the rest of the body. When the brain has to work harder to communicate to the body, then people experience symptoms like fatigue, anxiety, depression, stress, decreased immunity, headaches, and migraines.

She printed off my report from space and began explaining the nearly heaven-sent truth to why I felt overwhelmed. Before me, in black and white, I could see that my brain was working sixty-four percent harder than a healthy person's. She said it is normal for moms to have a higher percentage, but usually it's only around 20 percent–30 percent. Um, hello? Moms are in overdrive and that's normal? All moms everywhere need to understand that fatigue, stress, headaches, depression, and anxiety may honestly be a result of an exhausted brain. When you feel the "I suck at this" mentality creeping in, the problem is likely just in your head. What mom hasn't felt like her brain is about to explode? Of course, we would never let that happen because we would immediately feel guilty about leaving our children. So we hold it together until we may safely self-implode or take a hot bath or eat some chocolate.

My hope is that you can find bits of semantical chocolate in the coming chapters to inspire a healthier mind, body, and soul, propelling you into a thriving personal journey in the midst of some of the craziest years of your life. You got this, girl. You. Freaking. Got. This.

CHAPTER 14

Fuel Your Body and Soul

BREATHE

Don't skip this. If you haven't been doing this, you probably should. This is basic, I know. And maybe you feel like this should have been step number one in the beginning of the book. However, it was tough for me to start with breathing exercises. Taking a full breath in and letting it out slowly rarely calmed my mind enough to feel like it was effective. So what I found to be the most helpful was the 4-7-8 breathing technique—breathe in for four seconds, hold it for seven seconds, and then release the air for eight seconds. I like this technique because it made my mind stop and focus. I had to count. I could not mindlessly breathe deep breaths.

The practice of breathing and being aware of the oxygen in your body is so powerful. It brings a sense of calm when you breathe in through your nose and fill up your belly and chest, letting the oxygen pour into your extremities and every edge of your lungs and then gently breathing it out. There's a settling feeling that happens. A sense of peace and calm that can kind of take over. An awareness like—*Oh yeah, I'm human. I exist. I am taking up space in this world.* When we are wrapped up in the whirlwind, it's almost a spiritual experience to retract back from the chaos, to bring awareness to our soul and simply breathe. It's centering. Your body will thank you for the mini-break and the synergy.

SUNSHINE

The seasonal blues. The downer days. The glummy bummies. We all experience this in some fashion. Why not proactively ward off depression by soaking up much-needed vitamin D. Just a twenty-minute walk once a day can improve your life dramatically. One, it's exercise. Two, it gets the blood flowing and lymphatic system moving. Three, soaking up the sun has been proven to be the best way to absorb vitamin D. Dermatologist Richard Weller states in the article "Is Sunscreen the New Margarine?" that "avoidance of sun exposure is a risk factor of similar magnitude as smoking, in terms of life expectancy." His breakthrough research is proving that the big orange ball in the sky actually has a powerful connection to our body's ability to lower blood pressure, reduce the risk of cancers, improve mental health and circadian rhythms, and decrease inflammation. All of this by sourcing our bodies with what it needs to produce nitric oxide, serotonin, endorphins, and of course, Vitamin D. And it's free! A brisk walk, some freeze tag, sidewalk chalk art, tree climbing, a scavenger hunt with the littles—are all great ways to boost energy to help you get through the hustle of dinner and bedtime. You may not feel like taking twenty minutes to get the kids ready to go out the door, but this is one of those inconvenient habits where the benefits far outweigh the cost of not doing it. And like any new habit, eventually it will become second nature. You just need to get started.

GROUND

I talk a lot about habits to help you feel grounded in life. If you're having trouble experiencing this, I encourage you to literally sleep on the ground. When you lie down, feel the surety of the floor beneath you. It's constant. Always there. It never changes unless the dog pees on it, but even then, it stays. When life feels in flux or out of your control, this feeling, this connection is very comforting. The world is ever-changing but the earth is still earth. Feeling anchored in that steadiness is enlightening. Now if you're entirely opposed to this idea, take your shoes off and go for a walk outside. At the end of the day sometimes, I take my kids out on a barefoot walk. It helps my brain feel grounded to the world like I'm a part of it. This is extremely helpful for me when I have a lot on my mind or it's been a busy day. I can reel back my senses and remember what's truly important— to be present in this world because I exist. Barefoot walks are great. Maybe toss your toes in the water nearby. Or sunbathe at a park. Picnic with the kids and find shapes in the clouds as you lie down next to each other. It doesn't have to be weird or wacky. Just understand what your body needs to be its best and strongest version of you.

A great way to wrap a lot of these tips into one is by practicing yoga and meditation. And YouTube is the best free resource for this. Yoga with Adrienne is great if you're just starting out, and you don't feel comfortable joining the nearby yoga boutique. And Micheal Sealey has a ton of meditation clips to help with anxiety, overthinking, and stress. I usually listen to these if I'm having trouble falling asleep at night. You can also find clips on scripture, prayer, and worship meditation. You could even practice this outside.

Since you're focused on your breath, your posture, your thoughts, and the steadiness of the ground beneath you, yoga is a great way to ground yourself. The practice of controlling your movements in space brings a calmness to your mind and health to your body. Sometimes it's hard to stop and practice yoga and meditation. Life's demanding and time is a luxury. But don't worry. We will talk later about time management. Even a brief ten minutes will improve your wellbeing greatly.

PLAY

Life can too easily become a grind. Grocery lists, preschool prep, and gymnastics class ask a lot of us. Yes, the family needs food and healthy developmental curricular activities. But when we stop to play ninjas defending our playground village from the tree trolls, something awesome happens. We connect with our children. We tap into the youthful imagination that we had to lay to rest in order to fit into the societal norms of our growing age. There is an unexplainable peace in letting go of the to-do list task-master for five minutes, so your brain has a chance to engage in creative thought and to teach your little one to do the same. It's rejuvenating. It's restful. The endorphins that are released will boost your mood.

I realize we cannot forfeit all of life responsibilities to go play Barbies all afternoon. But what needs to be understood is that the time spent playing with your children could actually increase your energy, clear your mind, or settle your emotions such that you have more strength for the rest of the day.

So get out there and make some mud pies, jump in the sprinkler, and play tag with your kids. Side note: tag is a great workout! Do it outside and get some vitamin D for a double win. You will feel more connected to your kids by the mental and emotional bond made through playing. So good for your soul.

SELF-CARE LIST

I put a lot of emphasis on tapping into motherhood, but it is also important to address the deep need for quality self-care. No one can thrive in life without taking care of their own needs. You are fantastically created with unique passions that bring your soul to life. You may be in a season when you don't do much that speaks to that part of your heart. But I beg you, please don't forget about that part of yourself. Motherhood fills an entirely different space in our being, making us feel excited and full of love for our littles. But another part of your heart may eventually desire to feel alive again.

You may be thinking—*Brittany, I'm drowning in motherhood. I don't even know what my passions or hobbies are anymore.*

All I have to say is that life is a journey, a progression. You are not the same person you were a few years ago. As humans, we are constantly learning, growing, and evolving. Maybe tapping into a new passion will ignite your soul, and you would never have realized it until this point in your life.

Or maybe you used to be an ice skater as a young girl, and being on the ice made your heart soar and feel at peace. It provided that outlet to set aside the heavy demands of life, reach for deeper breaths, and feel connected to who you truly are. Maybe you play the piano, sing, knit, hike, or paint.

If you are struggling with ideas or want some inspiration on self-care, I have compiled a list of ideas that you can find here.

- Exercise
- Journal
- Play a musical instrument
- Paint your nails
- Punch a punching bag
- Take a hot shower or bath
- Go Shopping
- Listen to music
- Bake cookies
- Get a massage
- Dance
- Gardening
- Facials
- Make a list of blessings
- Perform a random act of kindness
- Rearrange the furniture
- Make a list of goals
- Learn a new yoga move
- Try a new recipe
- Get your hair done

I dare you to try something new. Boost your confidence through the spectrum of knowledge. There's a boldness that comes when you grow. And maybe that means taking up ice skating. Or maybe that means learning pottery. Do something for you that makes you feel alive. Find something that brings you joy. And do it every day if you can or once a week. It doesn't need to take up too much time. Make it fit your life and your family dynamic. Find something that's completely outside of mothering or caring for your home. Because you are more than just a mom. You are more than just a wife or an employee. Be you, girl.

EXERCISE

I'm not going to get all preachy on you here and tell you how you need to get up off the couch and put those yoga pants into some action. But I will say from experience that my mental health is directly proportional to exercising and that's likely true for you too. When I feel stronger in my own body, I feel more confident.

Hitting a goal or overcoming an obstacle transforms your perspective on yourself. You realize that you can actually do hard things. I'm not a health fitness coach. I'm just a girl who runs a couple miles and lift some weights sometimes. I'm talking to you like a friend.

Give yourself a fighting chance to thrive. Exercise is such a fantastic, tangible way to start. You can make clear goals and changes that impact your health and wellbeing. Start with a walk with a friend. Get your blood pumping and overcome the sluggish feelings that tear you down. If you want it badly enough, you will fight for it. Thrive, baby, thrive.

EAT BETTER

Again not going to jump on a soapbox here because I am definitely not a dietitian. I have personally done a few clean-eating challenges and have seen the tremendous impact that food has on my mental and physical health. I figured out how to serve my body instead of just feeding my body. In the process, I realized that I had been rewarding myself like a freaking dog at night time. I felt justified in eating my chocolate cake after a long day of dealing with crabby kids. But the enjoyment in the short term only made my life harder in the long term. My sugar addictions made me feel more on edge and anxious. I was living for my "next fix." I eventually got tired of letting food control so many of my thoughts and decisions. The truth was what I really wanted was more energy, less anxiety, and more confidence. Doing a clean-eating challenge helped me. Plus, I wasn't alone because I did it with a group. By breaking my bad habits, improving my gut and mental health, I not only lost weight, but my anxiety and impatience also decreased and I became less irritable.

It all came down to a choice. Do I want to thrive or not? I chose to fuel my body well by cutting out processed foods, sugar, dairy, soy, and gluten. Eating clean food gave me the strength that I needed to make better choices in other areas of my life. It gave me the mental clarity to feel more present and practice awareness. I felt grounded. I was able to maintain a better perspective in my day to achieve contentment, peace, and gratitude.

CHAPTER 15
Time Hacks

I'm going to start with a couple of practical ways to keep yourself encouraged and your mental health up. This is very basic stuff. But please keep in mind that I'm not a doctor, so none of this is clinical advice. If you are struggling, please see your family doctor.

Figure out what works for you. It may only be one or two things. Try something and if it doesn't work try something else. What works well for me may not be best for you. The good news is that our children will grow up and be OK even though they're all raised differently. Isn't that all we really want—for our children to be OK? Every mother's desire is for her children to grow up to be decent people that thrive in life.

So don't get overwhelmed here. Find one thing to zero in on. And go from there.

TIME VALUES

You could probably do this on a notepad or even on a nearby napkin if you're out on a hot date while reading this book. I provide a simple worksheet with clear steps in the free journal that I offered at the beginning of this book. If you have not claimed your journal, please stop and do that now. It will take two minutes. The goal is to get the worksheet done. You can come back to it as you work through this chapter and get a better grasp of how you would like to fill it out.

To break this mindset that you do not have time as a young mother, you will first have to have grace for yourself. Creating a value system for yourself and your family that you abide by every day will help the crazy days feel more intentional and important. And if your day throws you a curveball, you can be reassured that your life will continue within your values and never slip out of that alignment.

For instance, let's say health and physical fitness are big values to you and you plan to work out four times a week. But one morning your toddler suddenly can't stand wearing pants and throws a fit. Your spin class starts in t-minus fifteen minutes, and you can't seem to coerce your child into believing that putting on pants is actually super fun to do. You break out your love and logic parenting wand and offer him three marvelous choices to wear. Now that he gains control, he happily slips a pair on like everything is just as it should be. Mentally and emotionally exhausted, you head to the gym, drop off your little one in childcare and hop on a bike in spin class twenty minutes late.

This is real life. These things happen. But instead of pumping out an hour on the bike like you had hoped, you had to accept the reality of getting less time at the gym. But don't focus on the lack or what went missing. This will only feed negativity in your life. Consider it a win because you spent your time in such a way that it still aligned with your main values.

ALIGN WITH YOUR VALUES

So what are your standards? Start with three things that you value. Use the worksheet from this book to list out the important things that your family wants to focus on and pack your life full of things that align with your necessities. Narrow your focus. You may value twenty things. But at this time in your life, maybe dog rescuing, serving in a soup kitchen, and having a spotless house are not in your top three.

So after you figure out your top three or maybe even five things that you value in life, take a hard look at how you spend your time and your money. Do they line up with the things that you value? If they don't, look at what changes you can make.

EIGHTY TWENTY APPROACH

Break it down even further with the 80/20 approach. What takes up 80 percent of your time or energy but gives only 20 percent back to you in return? And you're not allowed to say your children. An example would be food. The time it takes to keep track of a running grocery list, meal plan, go to the grocery store, and then prep the food can be time-consuming. For some, this process is second nature, but for others, this could be considered a task that takes 80 percent of their time. It takes more energy to do this one thing, and once it's done, it does not reinforce a better measure of positive feelings—maybe 20 percent. For me, I was somewhere in the middle. I loved cooking, but I hated making grocery lists and going to the store. The main reason I started my first clean-eating challenge was for the preset grocery lists and recipes. I felt like I had my life back when I no longer had to come up with a meal plan and grocery list! I removed the task that took up too much mental energy from my life, so I could live more freely.

To evaluate this, write down all the things that take up your time. Include things like paying the bills, sorting the kids' toys, weekly playdates, and family dinners. Your list should hopefully have things that bring you joy as well as the hard stuff. Highlight the good things especially if they align with your values. If you can, eliminate the things that take up more time and give you less joy or energy in return to your family. If you can't give it up, outsource it or find another way to meet that need that takes up less of your time and energy. This way you can give more focus to the things that give you 80 percent in return, but may only take 20 percent of your focus.

PRINCIPLE OF MULTIPLES

Take the things you value and see how you can work it into the principle of multiples. Can you meet two or more of your values at once? Maybe health and friendship are in your top values. In this case, a multiplier would be going to the gym with a friend or walking the neighborhood together. Maybe it's getting together with a couple of friends to prep and swap healthy freezer meals one afternoon while the kids play together. Or maybe it's important for you to always be learning and to have quality time with your spouse. A multiplier would be to read a book together every night before you go to bed. The more values you can squish together in one activity, the better.

One of the great things about kids taking up so much of our time is that it helps us peel back the fluff in our schedules and take a hard look at what we truly feel is important. It will lead to a more fulfilling and purposeful life. An existence without purpose is just drifting. We were made for more.

BATCHING

Batching is doing the things that require a lot of energy at a time of day that you naturally feel more energized and vice versa. A high-energy task for me would be bill paying or paperwork. That requires a lot of mental energy from me with all the sorting and calculating. So I plan to do these tasks during my high-energy time. And tasks like doing dishes and laundry are low-energy output tasks for me. These are the mundane brainless chores. And I will schedule to do these chores when my brain is exhausted and doesn't want to have to think. This way I can get through the harder tasks faster and they are less life-sucking because I have scheduled them for the times that I have more energy to give.

BOUNDARIES

It's OK to say no sometimes. Know what your limits are. What's important is maintaining your balance and harmony. And that may mean missing a play date. It may mean not going to the girls' night this month because you need to spend time with your husband. If you are operating close to your limits, you're going to hit burnout mode fast. And when moms go up in flames, the whole house falls to ashes. You need to know yourself. And know what pushes you past your limit and steer clear of the fiery edge. Trust me, it will get easier in some ways the older your kids get. There will be more social time and you will be OK if you miss this month's Bunco gathering. Keep your boundaries in place so your family can thrive and you can avoid burnout.

OUTSOURCE

You probably know what things in your life drain you of energy versus what you're really good at. Outsourcing is a way to move things around so you can focus on what fills you up. There are a number of ways to do it. It could be as simple as setting up a carpool. Or watching your friend's baby one week and she watches yours the next. Maybe you have a friend who is a CPA and she's slammed each tax season. Maybe she'd love it if you brought over dinner for her and her family every Monday in March in exchange for doing your returns. Maybe you can change how you divvy up chores in your household. Perhaps your partner would be willing to trade bringing the kids to dance class for doing the laundry.

If it's in your budget, hire things out. If mopping and vacuuming are not your favorite things, hire a house cleaner. Snow blowing not up your alley, hire the teenager down the street. If you have a big birthday party coming up, hire a party planner. If you are not doing online grocery shopping, then you can look into that. Autopay everything, so you're not having to spend so much time dealing with bills every month.

There are a ton of online personal assistant companies out there who will help you with small tasks and big tasks. If you need to research good insurance companies but don't have time, hire it out. Outsourcing gives you power over your time. If these things aren't in your budget, maybe if you put in a couple of hours of overtime at work, you can have someone else do your cleaning. You can find ways to outsource or trade tasks. These little changes can give you the ability to focus on the things that you value. This is a huge hack that will hopefully allow you to spend more time doing things you enjoy.

ROUTINE

Create a routine for the normal adulting tasks. In order to keep things from becoming daunting and overwhelming, check them regularly if you can and take care of them. It's just all about creating a habit that is as instinctual as checking Facebook when you pick up your phone.

So instead of letting your dishes pile up in the sink, which I am very much guilty of, create the habit of just tossing them into the dishwasher as soon as you're done using them. And instead of checking your budget once a month, check it once a week or daily. Put cleaning supplies under every sink, so you can do a quick wipe through whenever needed. Sort the mail daily.

Creating small habits will impact your life in a big way because it alleviates the burden of a larger task later on.

LIMIT INTERRUPTIONS

They say it takes twenty minutes to return to the level of focus you were at prior to an interruption. If I add up all the interruptions correctly, I'm pretty sure I'm behind on all my thoughts by two years. The blissful days of having two consecutive thoughts together seem so long ago. And moms have enough interruptions with kids let alone email alerts. So do yourself a favor and take control of what you can. Aside from teaching your children not to interrupt, turn off the sound on your notifications. You don't need to check your email every half hour.

TIME BLOCK

If you want to take it to another level, schedule out time for social media and email. There are apps for this if you have a hard time not logging in. But feel a sense of empowerment because you're taking control of your life and you're not letting something else control you. There's so much information out there taking up our precious brain space. It uses energy we could be putting into things that are meaningful to us in our families. So conserve your brain energy and schedule these things out or take a fast from it. Do you really need social media in your life? Maybe you do. It is an incredible tool for communication, but it's often right in the center of our life. So optimize your time by conserving your brain energy and scheduling times where you will check your social media and email.

PROFESSIONAL HELP

Another suggestion would be to go see a doctor. Let's be real. Postpartum depression is hard. You're not crazy and you're not alone. Sometimes we just need a little extra help to get through a season and I promise you, it gets easier. There is no shame in this. You have to do what's best for you and your family. Talk to your family doctor. Schedule an appointment with a counselor. Drink some Starbucks. You're going to be OK. I promise.

CHAPTER 16
Final Remarks

If you can latch onto any takeaway from this book, let it be this—you are unmistakable. You are unmistakably loved as you are right now. You are wonderfully not perfect. And you are not alone. Motherhood is refining and very difficult at times. But it's this season of pruning that shapes us for the life ahead of us. Just as a tree must let go of its leaves to survive the brutal winter, we must embrace our mommy season knowing it has the power to train us up for something tremendous in the years to come . . . maybe the teenage years? And in all the trials, remember God is the source. Tap into him through prayer, gratitude, and reflection. He has given us all things that pertain to life! Girl, start tapping into the abundant life. Thrive, mama, thrive.

Tap In Like a Mother

If you feel inspired by any part of this book, but you are struggling to know how to spark your thriving life, I can help you. Join me in the Unmistakably Made Movement.

What's the Unmistakably Made Movement?

This is your fortitude, mama. It's a place for you to find rest, security, encouragement, truth, strength, and love. You don't have to struggle through this life alone. Feel empowered by the support and connection of others, and awaken what makes you unmistakably you for a more fulfilling and thriving life.

Book your UM SPARK call today
by going to this website!

http://bit.ly/UMSPARKCALL

Acknowledgments

Mom and Dad, without you I doubt I would have ever finished my rough draft. Thank you for taking on many of my life responsibilities while I tapped away at my computer for hours pouring my heart into this book. Thank you for believing in me and encouraging me to follow my dream of writing instead of just settling for a career elsewhere. Thank you for the faith that you both have and for spurring me on to do great things. I love you.

Shannon, my sister-in-love, thank you for spending so many hours pre-editing my book with me. Thank you for seeing the writing process for what it is and for not discouraging me from writing based on my awful first draft. Thank you for helping me find a way to make the book better. Your love and deep desire to see me do well in life is so real, and it overwhelms my heart. Thank you.

Tammie Stone, because of you, I started writing again. Thank you for speaking to me with such strong conviction and passion and for encouraging me not to wait until I "had more time" to write. Thank you for inspiring me to honor my God-given desire to write and to treat it as if it were my life calling responsibility. I no longer look at life the same since meeting you. I cannot thank you enough.

About the Author

As a little girl, I would climb our large maple tree and perch myself on a massive branch that split into two, making it the perfect resting spot. My siblings and I dubbed it the King's Throne. There I would write and read. If I didn't know what to write about, I would pretend to write by scribbling lines into a journal. However, it wasn't until years later when I attended the University of Missouri Kansas City, that I found my voice in writing and realized how much I truly enjoyed it.

A few years after graduating, I became a stay-at-home mom. Raising babies has been both wonderfully rewarding and extremely tough. But with great perspective and lots of grace, I continue to love my life in every season. I love encouraging other moms to find their passions and joys in life and to nurture them. Mamas are beautiful women with fantastically unique desires deep in their hearts. My hope as an author is to encourage women to see that their beauty and gifts are not without reason or cause.

Can You Help?

Thank You for Reading my Book!

I really appreciate all of your feedback, and I love hearing what you have to say.

Please leave me an honest review on Amazon letting me know what you thought of the book.

Thanks so much!
Brittany Churchill

You Can Write a Book Too!

Do you have a story and want to share it?

Do you want to leave a legacy for your family?

Do you want to teach something wonderful to the world?

Email me. For real.

I will help get you started on a proven success plan to write, produce, and publish your book.

brittany@brittany-churchill.com